Wanderers in Northamptonshire

Following in the steps of George Harrison,
writer, artist and poet (1876-1950)

by

John and Vera Worledge

Meridian Books

Published 1992 by Meridian Books

Reprinted with minor amendments 1998

© John and Vera Worledge 1992

ISBN 1-869922-18-2

Meridian Books
40 Hadzor Road
Oldbury
B68 9LA

Printed in Great Britain by MFP Design & Print, Manchester.

Contents

Kettering from Thorpe Malsor (Trail 2)

Preface

IN this book we follow the steps of the artist, writer and poet George Harrison (1876-1950) who toured the county of Northamptonshire in the 1920s, '30s and '40s, sketching and writing for a series of articles which appeared in Kettering and Wellingborough local newspapers.

We have lived in Northampton since before the 1960s expansion and the construction of the A1/M1 link, and a few years ago we felt that we would like to record for posterity some of the lovely aspects of our fair county. As we could neither draw nor paint we looked around for some way to record our thoughts and views. So we bought ourselves cameras, and John went to evening classes at Weston Favell school to learn the basics of photography with a fine teacher by the name of Neil Griffin. After traversing the county, with a couple of interviews on B.B.C. Northampton, we managed to photograph all 278 village churches.

"What next?", we asked ourselves. During our trips we had visited some lovely spots, so back we went to photograph the villages themselves before their beautiful vistas disappeared forever. Our researches involved several trips to the archives, then to Delapré Abbey and the Central Library, and it was during one of these visits that we first heard of George Harrison who lived in Kettering. He published several books of poetry, and his most famous book *A Wanderer in Northamptonshire* which consisted of the collected newspaper sketches, articles and poems. So a chase was on to find a copy of the book that was now out of print. We finally tracked down one copy in the 'Lanes' at Brighton.

The Spire of St Peter's,
Oundle (Trail 5).

What follows is a record of the first part of our travels around the county, following in George's footsteps and photographing today what George sketched yesterday. We have included many of George's sketches together with extracts from his writings and poems. We hope that you will agree with us that they give a fascinating picture of Northamptonshire as it was over half a century ago — and that our photographs will reassure you that much of the beauty that George so greatly admired still remains.

John and Vera Worledge.

George Harrison's reminiscences of his younger days
from his book
A Wanderer in Northamptonshire

MY birthplace was the old Workhouse Lane Kettering, in a cottage where now stands the building of the Northamptonshire Printing and Publishing Co. At the back of the cottage was the wood yard with its sawyers pit, and at the bottom lived Arch, the carrier. Near here, too, Meadows had his bake-house. Soon my people moved to Rockingham Road.

I remember as a boy, how, during the long summer evenings, the shadows of the sails from the old windmill used to pass over the shop window; and late in the autumn I have seen the corn harvested in the fields, where now stands the playground of the council school. A green led from Rockingham Road to the old mill, with the mill house and the buildings to the left. This was a typical country lane, where elderberry bushes grew on either side, and wild roses trailed in profusion amidst tall trees with a view of the mill beyond. It was painted by all artists of that time because of its rural simplicity and picturesque composition. I used to play on the grass opposite the mill, where now is Regent Street, and a walk to Milestone Lane (now Britannia Lane) used to seem a long way into the country in those days. In this lane, on the right hand side from Rockingham Road, was a pond partly hidden by willow and ash trees, which was a hunting ground for tiddlers whenever I had the courage to walk thus far.

The first school I attended was that of an old lady of the name of Brigstock, who lived in a cottage, one of a number under the name of Uppingham Terrace, opposite the shop in Rockingham Road. This old lady did little more than act as a nurse for small children. She would keep us quiet, I well remember, by scooping out with an old bone scoop the centre of an apple which she ate with evident relish, giving the best behaved child the rind.

After this I was sent to Gold Street which was at that time the infant department of the British School, under Miss Clark. The British School had overgrown its space, and this room was leased from the deacons of Fuller Church to relieve the congestion. Thus we boys and girls used to play in Sally Croft's entry, much to the annoyance of the old lady, who would chase us away with a broom. Arthur Studd had his foundry at the top of the entry, and Mr. Waiter Bell a corn chandler's shop at the bottom, where he followed Mr James, a furniture dealer. Mrs Smith kept a small shop opposite the school on the top of a number of steps, where I am afraid most of our halfpennies went in the purchase of delectable treacle toffee. At Fuller Church there was a splendid lending library, which was a real acquisition to us boys who early cultivated a love of good reading. I can still see those books, carefully covered with black cotton material, the work of the Misses Goodfellow. It was a real joy to go down to the library on a Saturday afternoon and select a book for the following week. Even now I marvel at the broad outlook of those people, who did not confine their selection of works to a kind which would repel, rather than encourage the love of reading. Mrs Henry Wood's works, I remember, were very much in favour, also the Brontë's, while books of travel were numerous and carefully selected, as were the works of eminent divines.

I was taken by my father to see Charles Bradlaugh who came to Kettering on the eve of the school board election. He was met and taken round the town in a procession headed by men carrying torches, and afterwards spoke at the Corn Exchange. My father told me to stand under the lamp which was in the centre of the Market Hill, so that he could find me when the meeting was over. The doors of the Corn Exchange were wide open owing to the large crowd, and I could distinctly hear Bradlaugh's voice, which, as many will remember, was of great volume and purity.

At this time I was at the British School, in School Lane, under Mr. Arthur Lenton, whose teaching was thorough, although his methods were severe. When I think of the conditions then prevailing I marvel that any results of value were possible. The crowded classrooms were filled with boys and girls, not always of the same age, and the rooms were uncomfortable during summertime and cold and ill-ventilated during the winter months. The curriculum was limited in scope, but what the teachers did have to teach, they were determined should be driven home in a manner too well impressed ever to be forgotten by the scholars for the rest of our lives. The playgrounds were very inadequate, which meant that before and after school hours most of the play took place in the street, entailing a good deal of clashing between the boys from the British School and the boys from the National School in the Horsemarket, then under the mastership of Mr S. J. Harding. These encounters became somewhat strenuous at times — particularly when snow was about — with resultant disfigurements to many on both sides.

Still, looking back to those days I recall that we were very happy and contented. We knew nothing of better schools, and certainly did not visualise the perfectly healthy

The young George Harrison
(with grateful thanks to Mr F Thomson).

conditions of the schools today. Most men of mature age remember the excellent results reflected in the afterlife of those who were fortunate enough to attend the British School. The conditions were bad, utterly bad, but by some means I have never quite understood, the results came, and these in larger proportion than in other bigger and better equipped schools.

I was in my thirteenth year when I left the British School, and then came the urge to draw and to paint. I was put in the hairdresser's shop where I had to stay until nine o'clock most days and eleven or eleven thirty on Saturdays. At this time there were no early closing days, but at every opportunity — mostly in the early mornings during spring and summer — I found my way into the country. This laid the foundation of my love for, and the familiarity with, my own county.

It was at this time that Sir Alfred East, T. C. Gotch and J. T. Nettleship, all of Kettering, were becoming famous in the art world. I was privileged to go often to see Sir Alfred East, who had a London studio in Spencer Street off Victoria Street, near the new Westminster Cathedral. My first visit was just after he had returned from Japan. He was holding a most successful exhibition of his Japanese drawings in Bond Street, where every individual drawing found a ready purchaser. Mr T. C. Gotch often dropped in to see me when he was visiting Kettering and it was through his influence, and the kindly help of Mr Frank Berrill (Manager of the Midland Bank) and of Mr Charles Henson that I was able to go to Antwerp in company with the late W. B. Gash, my first art master, where we spent the summer in hard and continuous study.

The wedding of George's daughter Hilda (Bosworth) on 15 September 1932. George is seated left and his wife next to him. The bridesmaid standing top right is George's niece Joan.

The years have rolled away in happy and continuous work. Many changes have come to Kettering, buι more have come to the countryside immediately surrounding it. The necessity of widening roads, and the making of arterial roads, the sin of ribbon building, and the felling of much fine timber without replanting has played sad havoc with parts of the county — the county that inspired Sir Alfred East and T. C. Gotch and laid foundation for their art. Sometimes I feel depressed regarding the future; at other times I have faith that good sense will prevail, and schemes of development be put forward, so that the county will move along the road of progress, maintaining the loveliness which has been an inspiration to so many in the past.

If strong public opinion is maintained, I see no reason why the county should not remain beautiful for all time, an inspiration to our people, and a joy in its beholding — a place of quiet peace, and fruitful toil, and where the aged may rest, and the children grow up in happy anticipation of healthy, good lives.

George Harrison. 1945.

George Harrison's obituary
(from the Kettering Leader)

Mr. George Harrison, 74 year old poet-painter died at his home, 270 Bath Road, Kettering, on the 31st. December 1950. His works were first published in this journal.

A hairdresser by trade, Mr. Harrison showed marked artistic ability from early school-days and in order that it should develop on the right lines a number of Kettering friends combined to enable him to study art at Brussels.

Landscapes were his particular interest and the countryside around his home town provided him with plenty of subjects, and his work soon attracted the attention of Sir Alfred East R.A.

Several notable art exhibitions have contained examples of his work, while year after year his paintings were included in the Kettering Art Exhibition, of which he was at one time secretary.

Mr Harrison was co-opted on the Kettering Education Committee in 1938 and did much to encourage an appreciation of art in local schools and donated a number of canvasses.

His love of the countryside also induced him to put his feelings on paper by means of the pen and, after earlier efforts in prose form, discovered a gift for poetry which he illustrated with pen and ink sketches.

It was the publication of these through the medium of this journal that won him recognition and praise from all parts of the county. Later these were collected and published in book form.

He leaves a widow and a daughter Mrs L. Bosworth. The funeral took place on Wednesday.

Northamptonshire

NORTHAMPTONSHIRE is nearly in the centre of England, and has a rather pleasant climate. It is bordered by seven counties, Leicestershire, Lincolnshire, Buckinghamshire, Oxfordshire, Warwickshire, Cambridgeshire and Bedfordshire. Since George travelled the county we have lost the Soke of Peterborough.

Northamptonshire was in early times the home of a Celtic tribe, the Coritani. The Roman occupation brought about great changes, many of which still have their effect today – for example, the Roman Watling Street traverses the county but now is better known as the A5. Towcester was a large Roman settlement (Lactodorum).

The Romans were followed by the Saxons, Danes and Normans, and much evidence of the presence of these invaders can be seen in our churches.

Saxon churches can be found at Brigstock, Brixworth and Earls Barton. There is Norman church architecture at Barton Seagrave, Geddington, Grafton Underwood and Rothwell. Norman church towers are notable in Spratton, Great Addington and Hargrave. Early English architecture appears at Strixton and Warmington.

The museum in Northampton houses many artifacts dating from the Roman, Saxon and Norman conquests.

The large tracts of forest once present drew many of the Kings and Queens of England to Northamptonshire. Rockingham, Whittlebury, Salcey and Yardley Chase were very popular with royalty.

The English Monarchy from William the Conqueror,
with the corresponding architectural periods.
(Illustrations by John Thomas Neville, RIBA)

Norman

William I (The Conqueror), 1066-1087
William II (Rufus), 1087-1100
Henry I, 1100-1135
Stephen, 1135-1154)

Norman, 1066-1189

West Doorway, St Giles, Northampton.
Norman.

Plantaganet

Henry II, 1154-1189
Richard I (Coeur De Lion), 1189-1199
John (Lackland), 1199-1216
Henry III, 1216-1272
Edward I, 1272-1307
Edward II, 1307-1327
Edward III, 1327-1377
Richard II, 1377-1399

Lancaster

Henry IV, 1399-1413
Henry V, 1413-1422
Henry VI, 1422-1461

York

Edward IV, 1461-1483
Edward V, 1483
Richard III, 1483-1485

Early English, 1189-1280

Decorated, 1280-1377

Perpendicular, 1377-1500

Tudor
Henry VII, 1485-1509
Henry VIII, 1509-1547
Edward VI, 1547-1553
Lady Jane Grey, 1533
Mary I, 1533-1558
Elizabeth I, 1558-1603

Stuart
James I (VI of Scotland), 1603-1625
Charles I, 1625-1649
Commonwealth declared on May 19th 1649
Oliver & Richard Cromwell, 1653-1659
Charles II, 1660-1685
James II, 1685-1688
William & Mary, 1689-1702
Anne, 1702-1714

Hanoverian
George I, 1714-1727
George II, 1727-1760
George III, 1760-1820
George IV, 1820-1830
William IV, 1830-1837
Victoria, 1837-1901

Saxe-Coburg
Edward VIII, 1901-1910

Windsor
George V, 1910-1936
Edward VIII, 1936
George VI, 1936-1952
Elizabeth II, 1952-

Early Tudor, 1500-1547

Late Tudor, 1547-1603

Stuart, 1603-1689

Hanoverian, 1689-1837

Piscina, St Kyneburga, Castor.
Early English.

Sedilia, St Kyneburga, Castor.
Norman.

St Mary's, Warmington.
Early English.

Milton Malsor.
Decorated.

St Mary's, Titchmarsh.
Perpendicular.

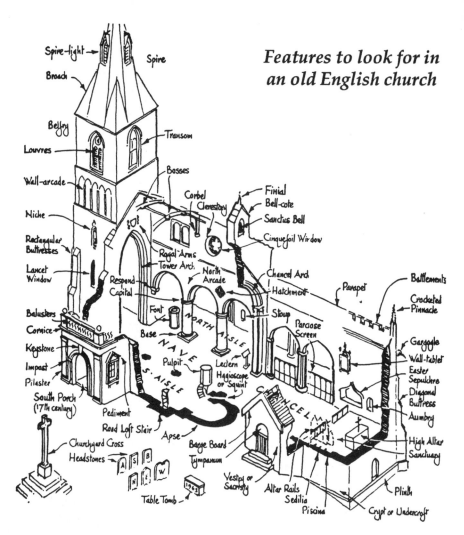

Features to look for in an old English church

Drawn by Anthony S B New and reproduced with his kind permission.

Dedications

We would like to dedicate this book to:

Dorothy Webb, Mary Exley and Joan Carnell, the granddaughters of George Harrison, without whose help this work would have not got off the ground; Renée Goodliffe, aunt to George's granddaughters; Our wonderful grandchildren, Katy and George.

A Northamptonshire Orchard.

Acknowledgements

WE wish to record our grateful thanks to the following:

Neil Griffin, whose chance remark at a photography class led us on our trails around the county;

The Northampton and Kettering Libraries for their extensive help in tracing George Harrison's granddaughters;

Simon Thortons (Jewellers) of Kettering for their help with the addresses of the granddaughters;

Joan Carnell, Mary Exley and Dorothy Webb, the granddaughters of George Harrison, who gave us permission to use George's works in our book;

The staff of the Kettering Art Gallery for showing us the paintings by George that are stored and displayed at the gallery;

Malcolm Robinson of the Kettering Reference Library for his unstinting help in discovering notes on George in the reference library;

The Editors of the *Kettering Leader and Telegraph* and *The Citizen*, and to Carmel Crawley of the Archive Department, for their help and permission to publish George's work for the papers from the 1930s and the 1940s;

Jennifer Fell of Hellidon for her advice on our manuscript;

Ted Eassom of Rothwell for acquiring the 1928 poems and sketches of George Harrison and for his help in obtaining two of George's paintings;

The *Northampton Chronicle and Echo* Newspapers for permission to publish their photographs of the 800 year Charter celebrations;

Rachel Watson, County Archivist, for her help with the Charter photostat and her advice in the preparation of our book;

Mrs Jean Holt of Harrington, who sent us a 1927 book of George's poems;

Edwin John Storry of Broughton, who gave us a lovely pen and pencil sketch by George Harrison;

John Thomas Neville R.I.B.A., who did the marvellous drawings of the architectural periods of our churches;

Our dear friends at Corby, Georgina and Bernard Barry, for their gift of Nickolaus Pevsner's book on Northamptonshire;

Mrs Odell for her help with the initial photostats for our manuscript;

Prontaprint of Northampton for their help with the final photostats for our manuscript;

Finally to the people of Northamptonshire who gave us so much help as we toured the county;

Vera and John Worledge

WEEKLEY.

By GEORGE HARRISON.

COTTAGES IN WET LANE, WEEKLEY.

When the toil of the day is over,
  And the dusk of the evening falls,
When from his green enfolded cover,
  The brooding partridge calls:
There is a place where I love to linger,
  Near to the noisy, broad highway,
To watch the sun with magic finger
  Spill the last gold threads of day.

Pure the hue of the sunset burning
  On the trees, and on Warkton's tower,
The narrow stream that with every turning
  Silvers some leafy bower;
Flows through the meadows lush and golden,
  By the willows, and grey between,
The road-way bridge moss grown and olden
  Stands by trembling rushes green.

Flutter the moths above the grasses,
  Dim are they in the fading light,
The last faint glow of crimson passes
  Into the coming night.
Far in the North one star point beaming,
  Softly hued in the quiet sky,
On Grafton-road huge headlights gleaming
  Mark the motors flashing by.

And the eye of the June day closes
  O'er the fields and distant town;
A silver film of light reposes
  Where the winding stream flows down
To meet the full moon slowly sailing
  Into a mystic bowl of blue,
Like phantoms lost the white mists trailing
  Down the dark elm avenue.

The original of Mr. Harrison's drawing can be purchased for 10/6, which sum
will be given by Mr. Harrison to the Kettering and District General Hospital.
Application should be made to the office of this journal.

*One of George Harrison's original contributions to
the Kettering Leader as it appeared on 1 July 1927.*

George at work painting in the field by his favourite village, Warkton.

Trail 1
Kettering • Boughton House • Weekley • Warkton • Geddington • Rushton • Rothwell

Kettering

W E have visited Kettering on several occasions and, as we climb up from the station, we always view with awe, at the top of the hill, the magnificent Perpendicular spire of the church of St Peter and St Paul which rises to 179 ft. All around the church are signs of Kettering's history including the lovely seventeenth century Manor House, built of ironstone, and now housing the museum. The Public Library, the Sir Alfred East Art Gallery and the Tourist Information Centre are close by — and also a substantial car park. Just opposite the Art Gallery are Sawyer's Almshouses dating from 1688.

Grant of Arms by the Earl Marshall and Hereditary Marshall of England, dated 26th September 1938.

Kettering was not without its great men and, as he recorded in his reminiscences (p. viii), George Harrison rubbed shoulders with artists Sir Alfred East, T. C. Gotch and J. T. Nettleship. Also well known was William Knibb who was educated at Kettering Grammar School and spent most of his life in the West Indies as a missionary. He was prominent in the fight against slavery and is remembered by Kettering in its town crest which includes a slave with broken shackles.

Another local worthy was William Carey, one of the founders, around 1729, of the Baptist Missionary Society.

Well known in the town is the magnificent Tresham College: this has a fine theatre which is well used by the local community. The Kettering Operatic

Society regularly performs there: among its members are George's granddaughters who, like their grandfather, have wonderful singing voices.

We found the following description of the borough's arms in George's book:

Shield — The hide is indicative of the leather used in the chief industry — the manufacture of boots and shoes. The waved lines within the circles are "Heraldic Fountains" and symbolise the formation of the Baptist Missionary Society at the Mission House in Lower Street in 1792. The birds within the circles are taken from the arms of the Watson family of Rockingham who, with the Montagu family, are Lords of the Manor of Kettering. The cross between the circles is from the arms of the See of Peterborough under the Ecclesiastical jurisdiction of which See Kettering comes.

Supporters — The Griffin reguardant is from the Arms of the Montagu family who, with the Watson family, are Lords of the Manor of Kettering. The figure in black with the broken chain symbolises the pioneer and triumphant work of William Knibb in the cause of the freedom of Slaves. Knibb was born in Market Street, Kettering in 1803.

Crest — The Flames and Iron Chain encircling them represent the Iron-Ore Industry, and the skein of silk below the chain, with the heraldic mantling between the Supporters and the Crest, relate to the clothing industry. The helmet and mantling are incorporated by the College of Heralds in all Arms granted to Boroughs.

Motto — *Progressio et Concordia* (Progress and Concord.)

A well known feature of Kettering is Wicksteed Park which is run by a trust created by Charles Wicksteed who gave this park to the children of Kettering. He founded an engineering works making ploughshares and farm implements,

Lakeside Railway, Wicksteed Park.

The railway is still a popular feature of Wicksteed Park.

and made his fortune by inventing a speed change gear. He bought a grass field near Barton Seagrave on the outskirts of Kettering and turned it into a pleasure park for the people of Kettering. If you look in the gardens in the park in front

The people of Kettering enjoying Charles Wicksteed's legacy.

of the pavilion you will find a statue of a little brown terrier dog called Jerry who was a constant companion to Charles Wicksteed.

George wrote a poem *Early Morning: The Wicksteed Park*. Here are two verses:

Upon the surface of the lake a gleam
Of silver scintillates, the breezes stir
The waters, and the little eddies beam
With twinkling glory light as gossamer.

The swings stand idle now, no painted boat
Moves to the music of dripping oars,
The little island seems to softly float
Far from the purple of the shelving shores.

Boughton House

BOUGHTON HOUSE creates the impression of being a French Chateau. This influence comes from the time when the first Duke of Montagu, who built the house, was Ambassador to the Court of Louis XIV. The house contains a very good collection of French furniture. The avenue of trees was planted by the Second Duke.

Boughton House.

Boughton House is well worth a visit – this is what George wrote when he came here:

The lovely, unspoilt villages of Weekley and Warkton lie just outside Kettering, off the Stamford Road. Their intimate connection with the great estate of Boughton Park has preserved their simplicity and enhanced their beauty. Their churches have superb monuments to the Montagus of Boughton, who built Boughton House and developed the park into a miniature Versailles. Much of their famous garden has disappeared, but the whole surrounding countryside is beautified by the noble avenue of elms (*that was before Dutch Elm disease*) mingled with some limes, which run in all directions for a total length of thirty miles or so. They were planted by the second Duke of Montagu, known as John the Planter, a man of great kindness, who established one of the first homes for old and decrepit animals. Boughton House passed by marriage to the Douglas-Scott family, who took the name Montagu-Douglas-Scott. (*Boughton House is now the home of the Duke of Buccleuch.*)

Two verses of George's poem *Boughton House* present a nice picture of the house and its surroundings:

Secluded near to broad highway
'Midst ancient trees and fertile lands,
With mossy stones grown old and grey
This regal home of Beauty stands.
The hum of sure encroaching town
Breaks not its tender calm serene;
Still flows the stream o'er gravels brown,
Still sigh the bending rushes green.

Old marks remain of feudal years,
The draw-bridge and the sunken moat,
Those emblems of man's primal fears
Now happily of days remote.
The remnants of fair avenues
That "John the Planter" wisely spread,
Each Springtime flaunt their changing hues
And wave their bud points overhead.

Weekley

In the churchyard at Weekley is the simple grave of J. Alfred Gotch, M.A., a former President of the Royal Institute of Architects and Vice-President of the Society of Antiquaries, a Justice of the Peace for Northamptonshire, and Charter Mayor of Kettering in 1938. His forbears established the footwear industry of Kettering in the eighteenth century and were also its leading bankers. Of his three brothers, Thomas Cooper Gotch, R.I. was a noted painter of children, Davis Gotch was Secretary to the County Education Committee, and Alderman Henry Gale Gotch, J.P., was the leader of the musical life of Kettering.

The handsome Almshouses adjoining the churchyard of St Mary's, Weekly, were founded by Edward, first Baron Montagu, in 1611. Near the orchard of the Almshouses lies the charming old schoolhouse built by Nicholas Latham in 1624, and now thoroughly restored.

The fine stone and thatched cottages with good front gardens, and the vicarage tastefully designed by Sir A. Blomfield are also notable.

George Harrison.

We found the village hardly changed when we visited it in the summer of 1991. We had a very enjoyable cup of tea at the tea rooms/post office sitting in the glorious sunshine and having a nice chat with the lady in charge.

Cottages in Wet Lane, Weekley.

The cottages are little changed today – but the lane is renamed Wash Well Lane.

Sadly, most of the beautiful Weekley Woods were laid waste for Corby Steel Works in the 1950s. This is how George knew them:

I knew no woodlands half so sweet,
Nor grass more lush for tired feet,
I wondered did the fairies play
In green recesses hid away,
Or Pan pipe forth his jocund tune
Among the rustling reeds of June,

Warkton

HERE we came to George's favourite village, and we agree very much with his feelings. The fifteenth century church of St Edmund houses the monuments to the Montagu family from nearby Boughton House. George wrote some fine poems to the village, and they describe it not only as it was

Warkton from the meadows.

then but also, happily, as it remains today:

> From thy green upland's slender height,
> The little pathways wander down
> To meadows fringed by winding stream,
> Where elm and drooping willow meet,
> And shady pools at noontide seem
> A woodland fairies' green retreat.

Warkton today.

Another poem has the poet in reminiscent mood — but displaying a touch of sadness:

> Thy peaceful beauties were my earliest joy
> And source of my repose, when but a boy.
> I sought each pleasant nook, each green recess,
> Each rural view of quiet comeliness.
> Here, first my youthful love of art was born,
> Those high ideals which leave me now forlorn.

In *The New Year* he pictures the serenity and peace of the village:

> Here gently borne to me the joyful sounds
> Of Warkton Church bells ringing. Dimly glow
> The patient stars, and tranquil peace abounds
> To bless the passing hours, that softly flow
> Into eternity of vanished time,
> That beats with measured tread its ceaseless rhyme.

Geddington.

THE village of Geddington is rich and varied. To the archaeologist it is particularly attractive. The old bridge south of the church crosses the Ise stream almost in the centre of the village. The diversion of the stream to the

Medieval Bridge, Geddington.

The bridge as we saw it.

mill, and the building up of the banks of the stream, were done by the early Romans, who also mined for iron ore in this district. Many early Roman remains have been found in the iron ore workings.

The bridge, which is quite narrow, dates from about 1250. It has five good arches, with long approaches from either side. There are three cut waters pointing up-stream which form shelter for foot passengers on the bridge-way. The two northern arches are the oldest, one of the others being quite modern.

George Harrison

The village is well known for its monument which stands in the centre of the village — the Queen Eleanor Cross, one of three left in the country. The others are at Hardingstone, and Waltham Cross in London. These are in memory of Queen Eleanor, wife of Edward I, who died in 1290. It was Queen Eleanor who sucked the poison from a wound which her husband sustained on his crusade at Acre, risking her life for his. They lived

The Eleanor Cross at Geddington.

happily for another thirty years before she died at Harby in Nottinghamshire. The king was on his way to see her when she became very ill, but he arrived too late. He laid her heart in Lincoln Cathedral. Then followed the funeral march to London, some 150 miles, stopping at twelve places *en route*. Of the twelve crosses erected by Edward alas only the three mentioned are now standing. The one at Charing Cross is a replica.

The motor car was already having an effect on Geddington when George was writing:

Much of thy rural charm has passed away
In these thy later years; oft now heard
The roar and rush of motors through the day
To blend so strangely with the song of bird,
The sigh of falling rain among the trees,
The low of cattle and the hum of bees.

Rushton

RUSHTON is the home of the Tresham family. They built Rushton Hall over six hundred years ago. In the fifteenth century William Tresham and his sons were Speakers in the House of Commons. The father was killed by the Lancastrians; the son, Thomas, grew up in the Court of King Henry VI and finally lost his head on the block.

The sixteenth century was the heyday of the family. There was Thomas the Grand Prior, Thomas the builder, and Francis who became mixed up in the Gunpowder Plot. Thomas the Prior was a good friend of Mary Tudor – for his help she revived the Order of St. John and made him its Grand Prior, and he sat in the House of Commons. He died peacefully at the time of the Spanish

The Triangular Lodge, Rushton.

North-East Corner of Rushton Hall

... and as we saw the Hall.

Armada and was succeeded by his grandson Thomas, aged fifteen years. Thomas was much concerned with religion. He harboured the famous Jesuit, Edmund Campion, and for this was sentenced to seven years imprisonment. It was Thomas (by now Sir Thomas Tresham) who built the famous Triangular Lodge and the Market House at Rothwell, and also the New Bield at Lyveden. His son Francis was the Tresham who became involved in the Gunpowder Plot – it was thought that it was he who wrote to one of his friends warning him not to attend Parliament on that fateful day, so leading to the plot being uncovered. For his part he was imprisoned in the Tower, but he died there before he was brought to trial.

Rushton Hall is today a school for blind children with additional handicaps and run by the R.N.I.B. It is now being tastefully restored by the Institute, and we thank them for their kind permission to photograph where George sat and did his sketch.

The Triangular Lodge was erected in 1593-1595. Everything is three sided, gables, floors, windows and pinnacles. It is thought to be a symmetrical presentation of the doctrine of the Holy Trinity.

The unique structure of Lyveden New Bield was built between 1595-1605 as a garden lodge for Sir Thomas's main residence, Lyveden Old Bield. Sir

Lyveden New Bield, between Brigstock and Oundle

Thomas, whose son Francis was imprisoned in connection with the Gunpowder Plot, was a deeply religious man with a great knowledge of architecture. His strong Catholic beliefs led to many years of persecution and financial hardship, with long periods of heavy fines and imprisonment enforced by the Protestants. However the building was to be his celebration of Christ.

Built of local oolitic limestone in the shape of a cross, it was never finished and has remained as you see it since Sir Thomas died in 1605. It was bought by the National Trust in 1922 together with 28 acres of lands including the water gardens, now alas overgrown. You can see these on your right as you walk up the farm track from the road. As we looked through the trees we disturbed around a hundred resting ducks on the bank

Rothwell

THE busy little manufacturing town called Rothwell or Rowell was a Royal Manor at the Norrnan Conquest; it had a castle, fortified walls, a nunnery, and one of the finest churches in the County. The castle and the walls have disappeared. The spire of the church fell down in the seventeenth century but the top of the spire was reset on the stair turret on the north side of the tower.

Elizabeth's reign brought new architectural beauties. John Thorpe designed for Sir Thomas Tresham a fine Market House, which remained roofless for 300 years, until it was skilfully completed by J. Alfred Gotch in 1895. The stonework is most delicately wrought and there are eighty-nine

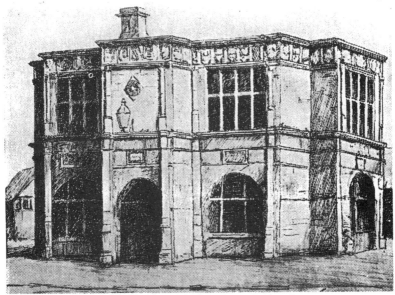

The Tresham Market House, Rothwell

... and our picture.

Coats of Arms of great Elizabethan families round the cornice. Near by is the pleasant Jesus Hospital, founded by Owen Ragsdale, founder also of the Grammar School. The Hospital is still in full use for elderly men of the Town. Holy Trinity Church, the longest in the County, is remarkable for its

Old Nunnery House, Rothwell.

When we visited the Old Nunnery it was undergoing repairs to the chimneys. Note that the thatch is still in place on the right.

size and good lighting. There are four fine old brasses, and a remarkable bone-crypt contains the bones from 4,000 skeletons. Rothwell has an annual fair, which is still opened by the ceremonial reading of a Charter at 6 a.m. on the Monday following Trinity Sunday. Rothwell was one of the early centres of Congregationalism, the "Independent" Church having had a continuous existence since 1656. In 1691 it appointed Deaconesses, and in 1735 could accommodate a thousand worshippers.

The cottage architecture of Rothwell, like that throughout the County, is varied and beautiful. The principal material is the ruddy yellow ironstone, with deep thatch or yellow Collyweston tiles. The deep dormers in the thatch are a notable feature of the Northamptonshire cottage.

George Harrison

We wonder what George would say today if he could see the swath of the M1-A1 link cutting through our fair county!

Trail 2

Desborough • Thorpe Malsor • Loddington • Broughton •
Cransley • Pytchley

Desborough

THE grave of a Saxon lady was found here at Desborough. We cannot doubt that she was a Christian for the symbol of her faith was interred with her. This was an exquisite necklace of thirty seven beads and a pendant cross of gold — one of the earliest Christian crosses found in the country. It is now in the British Museum.

Church of St Giles, Desborough.

In another grave was a bronze mirror with an elaborate handle six inches long and engraved with the lovely spiral design of Celtic art. This cherished possession of a woman of a still earlier period is also in the British Museum.

The Desborough mirror. (By courtesy of the Trustees of the British Museum.)

Thorpe Malsor

The distant town lies like an isle of dreams,
Above the glories of a full green sea,
The smoke from furnace chimneys, drifting far,
Floats lazily across the sky of blue,
Forms into serried lines, and melts away.

THIS is George's scene of Thorpe Malsor. Alas!, the cottages are no more, but we did meet Mr. Goodman, aged 80, who has lived in the village all his life and has the original sketch, given to him by George, hanging in his living room. He was born in the middle cottage in the scene. The out-houses were the village store and the end cottage was the home of the village carpenter — you can just make out the shed in the garden where he stored his timbers.

Mr Goodman, reminiscing about his younger days in the village, told us that a bottle of ginger pop was a halfpenny (old money) and when he took the bottle back he got a farthing. In 1918 a bottle of beer cost a penny.

A bit of history that came to light dealt with the Maunsell family. A member, who fought at the Battle of Naseby, was wounded and was left for dead. The body was about to be stripped preparatory for burial when a young lady, the daughter of an apothecary, finding the hand soft, exclaimed, "This certainly

One of the old village springs, was dated 1589 (the time of the Spanish Armada). This spring (now covered) is dated 1891. If you listen closely you will hear the water running through the drain on the right.

Thorpe Malsor Church

was a gentleman". She further observed that she felt a pulse, and consequently that he was not dead. She put off her petticoat, and wrapping him in it, had him conveyed to a neighbouring village, where he recovered. Mr Maunsell being thus providentially rescued from death, lived for some years afterwards, and employed the young woman as a housekeeper till the time of his death, when he left her a handsome annuity.

The thirteenth century doorway to the church of St Leonard's, Loddington. According to Arthur Mee the projection moulding over the door was probably protecting a sculpture, long disappeared.

Loddington

THE Hall was built in the seventeenth century by the Kynnesman family. Although altered during the centuries it still retains the great hall with the lovely Jacobean panelling.

In the church (p. 21) there is a most intriguing wall tablet, in the memory of a rector's son. He was killed by a musket ball while in General Abercrombie's army when they defeated the French near Alexandria in the first half of the last century.

Broughton

AT Broughton are memories of Tudor days. In the church in a niche is a marble bust of Harrold Kynnesman — he was Treasurer to Queen Elizabeth I's army, led by the Earl of Essex, when it was sent to quell the Irish

Broughton Church.

Broughton Church today.

rebellion. He lost favour with the Queen and finished up with his head on the block.

While photographing the church one afternoon we met Mr. John Storry who lives opposite the church. We spent quite a few lovely afternoons sitting in his farmhouse kitchen chatting about George and the old times. He kindly gave us a pen sketch that George had given to him (p. 27).

Cransley

Green fields enfold thee with a soft caress,
And little streams meander where they will
By shelving bank and reed-fringed cool recess,
Where fragrant flowers their tender fragrance spill.

THE noble thirteenth century church of St Andrew, Cransley, has become a shrine of Anglo-American friendship. A carol service broadcast from there one Christmas forged the first links of comradeship with the United States. Closer bonds were woven during the Second World War. The vicar, the Rev. Grenville Cooke M.A., Mus. Bac, F.R.A.M. offered to conduct an American Thanksgiving service for troops in the Midland area. Later, American soldiers presented the church with a stained-glass window, which was set in an early Perpendicular window facing west towards America, and is protected by tall gilded gates of wrought iron, presented earlier by Mr and Mrs Alan G. Timpson, of Kettering. The flags of both countries hang in the church. A book containing the signatures of the American soldiers who gave the window is shrined in the church.

The Churchill Window. It was placed in the west wall of the church so that it would face America.

The cranes in the Arms on other windows were emblems of the Cransley family (*herons used to nest in the osier beds near the church*); there are fine brasses of 1515 and 1516 to the Dallyson family, and one of 1602 to Edward Barnwell. The hall stands near the church.

George Harrison. 1946.

The lovely stained-glass window in the church is known as the Churchill Window. It represents a pictorial record of six historical occasions associated with the history of Britain and America, the centre panel being dominated by St Michael clasping the sword of faith watching over a soldier of each country holding hands. At the unveiling ceremony this was enacted in real life by Lance Corporal Francis J. Stapleton of Kettering who, as a boy worshipped at St Andrews church, and Private First Class Bernard Jackson of Vicksburg Mississippi.

The side panels depict John Cabot, on his voyage from Britain to America in 1497; the Pilgrim Fathers, making the Mayflower Compact in 1620; William Penn organising a treaty with the Indians in 1631; Thomas Hooker proclaiming the Hertford Constitution in 1639; Abraham Lincoln making his Gettysburg Address; and last but not least the conference held on the high seas to discuss the Atlantic Charter between Sir Winston Churchill and

Panel in the Churchill Window recording the meeting with President Roosevelt in 1941.

Franklin Roosevelt, President of the United States, in 1941. It is truly a magnificent window and a permanent reminder, not only of the men who flew from the airfield but a memorial to many of their comrades who never returned from bombing missions over Europe and Germany. Another interesting point is that it is claimed to be the only stained glass window showing someone smoking, in this case Sir Winston Churchill and his cigar.

Pytchley.

It stands on a breezy upland,
So near to busy town,
Where the corn fields and the stubbles
To verdant fields slope down,
And the little path goes winding
Through the meadows gold and brown.

The entrance to Pytchley Village.

NEAR Pytchley there lived, in Saxon times, the Royal Huntsman to Penda, King of Mercia (circa AD577-655). About 1760 kennels were built at Pytchley for the pack of hounds which John, Earl Spencer, kept here for half the season, hunting for the rest of the season from Althorp. The old Elizabethan Hall at Pytchley, built by a member of the Isham family, which resided there before the move to Lamport, was for about 60 years from 1761 the home of the famous Pytchley Hunt Club which has made this village famous in sporting circles throughout the world. The Pytchley kennels are now at Brixworth.

George Harrison.

The keeping of hounds was permitted in order to control vermin in the district.

Because of the growth of trees on the Kettering side where George did his sketch we have taken our photograph of All Saints Church, Pytchley from the south.

Midsummer Glory. George's original sketch was given to us by Mr John Storry of Broughton. (See p. 23)

Trail 3
Burton Latimer • Barton Seagrave • Cranford • Twywell •
Grafton Underwood

Burton Latimer

Church of St Mary and school house, Burton Latimer.

THE church of St Mary at Burton Latimer contains a fine series of Elizabethan wall paintings. There is also a brass portrait of Margaret Bacon, a seventeenth century lady of the manor; she wears a mantle with a baby lying at her feet.

The lovely building to the west of the church was a Jacobean schoolhouse founded by one Thomas Burbank in the reign of Queen Elizabeth I but built in 1662 and, according to Nikolaus Pevsner, converted to a private residence in 1972.

We found this quotation in Whellan's *History, Gazetteer and Directory of Northamptonshire, 1849* — which shows that carpets were once made here:

Messrs. Davis and Co's worsted mill which burnt down in October 1848, when machinery, etc., to the amount of £7,000 was destroyed and has lately been rebuilt, and when in full production will weave 16,000 yards of carpeting per week and employ 400 staff.

Barton Seagrave

IT seems that 'progress' was already affecting the rural calm of Barton Seagrave when George visited here:

Barton, long years ago, seemed far away,
A sylvan spot to fill a summer's day,
When I would muse beneath the changing skies,
Where nought disturbed of toil or traffic's noise,
Now modern villas, set in orderly rows,
Blend strangely where the nodding harebell blows.

The Church of St Botolph, Barton Seagrave is Norman, though altered over the years. Close by are mounds and moat – all that remain of a castle built by Sir Nicholas Seagrave in the reign of Edward II.

A distinguished inhabitant of Barton Seagrave was the historian John Bridges who wrote a history of Northamptonshire..

"It was esteemed one of the best county histories that was ever published. The materials for it was collected by Mr Bridges with great labour, and at an expense, it is said, of several thousand pounds, but he died before these materials could be compiled. The work was thrown into its present shape by the Rev. Peter Whalley, and published in the year 1791."

From Whellan's *History, Gazetteer and Directory of Northamptonshire, 1849.*

Early Norman Doorway, St Botolph's Church, Barton Seagrave.

Cranford

A village set just off the road,
With shady lanes and meadows green,
Where vans and cars with rumbling load
Through twinkling shadows pass, between
Tall elms, and hedgerows white with may,
Small cottages with gardens sweet,
And overhanging roofs of grey,
Which shield from bitter cold and heat.

THE tiny roadside village of Cranford has two churches, a hall set in a noble park, and a lovely old Manor House with a fine seventeenth-century staircase.

Cranford under snow, sketched in 1935

...and as we found it on a fine summer's day.

One of the fine carvings on the choir stalls depicting Livingstone's Africa (by permission of the Kettering Leader and Telegraph).

A resident of Cranford was the Rev. Eusebius Paget, author of the *The History of the Bible* and other works. He was born here in the reign of Queen Mary and died in London in 1617.

Cranford seems as peaceful now as it was when George sat here to sketch the church and hall. The A1-M1 link has moved most of the traffic away from the village — one road development to be thankful for!

Twywell

WE cannot pass Twywell without telling you the amazing story of David Livingstone. He was a great friend of the Rev. H. Waller who was the rector of Twywell.

When David Livingstone died in Africa on May Day 1873 he was found by his two faithful servant boys Sisi and Chuma. It was Susi who decided that they would bring his body home to England to be buried in the home of the white queen (Queen Victoria) so that his own people could honour him. After embalming his body and planting his heart under a tree in a place called Chitambo, they wrapped his body in bark and carried it 800 miles to the sea, overcoming many hazards on the way. The body was carried on a pole and at one place they had to disguise it as a bale of cotton to enable them to pass through a chief's territory.

Displayed in the church are pieces of the bark that covered the body and pictures of the two boys.

They stayed at the rectory while the Reverend Waller researched the chronicles of Livingstone which the boys brought back with them.

David Livingstone was buried in Westminster Abbey.

Susi and Chuma proved invaluable to the Rector with their help and knowledge of Africa and the doctor's work and life — they also brought back seeds gathered by Livingstone and these were planted in Kew Gardens.

One of the boys went back to Africa. The other stayed in England and later married a French girl: they had two sons and one of them married a Twywell girl.

(*These notes are from the Twywell church pamphlet, with grateful thanks.*)

Susi and Chuma in their traditional dress.

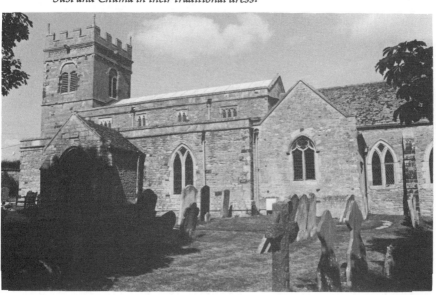

Church of St Nicholas, Twywell.

Grafton Underwood

The sun and shade at Grafton
Play in the village street,
And the chestnuts and the aspens
Over the waters meet;
The old-world flowers in the garden
The eyes of the strangers greet.

The bridge at Grafton Underwood as George sketched it.

GRAFTON UNDERWOOD was the main base of the United States Air Force during the Second World War from 1942 until 1945. We came here looking first for Quentin Bland who lives at the Post Office, for it is to Quentin we owe most of what we are about to tell you.

After getting the key from Quentin at the Post Office we made our way to the church of St James where we were able to see the magnificent stained glass window in the side chapel.

The Memorial Window (p. 36) is dedicated to the 384th Bombardment Group (Heavy) and was dedicated on Saturday May 21st 1983 in the presence of Her Royal Highness Princess Alice of Gloucester.

From the leaflet *Coming Home*:

This window is dedicated before God in remembrance of those who gave their lives for freedom during World War II while serving at Grafton

The bridge today.

Underwood from 1942 until 1945, especially those members of the 384th Bombardment Group (Heavy) of the 8th United States Air Force.

The significance of the memorial window dedicated to the members of the 384th Bombardment Group (Heavy) is that it is placed in the parish church of St James the Apostle as a permanent reminder of the efforts of the members of the 384th in World War II, and in particular the 1579 members lost while in combat whilst flying from the airfield here at Grafton Underwood.

The blue sky represents the arena in which the 384th saw combat and many fought their last fight. The white cliffs of Dover are symbolic in the sense that these were the first sight of England the aircrews had upon returning from combat over Europe. The crossed flags signify the combined efforts of both cou.ntries in the defeat of the common enemy during World War II. The four badges at the top of the window are of the 544th, 545th, 546th, and 547th squadrons, and the shield below is of the 384th Bombardment Group (Heavy) itself. The motto "Keep the show on the road" came from the Deputy Group Commander Major Seldon McMillan whilst he was in a P.O.W. camp after being shot down on one of the group's earlier missions.

The Memorial Window.

The aircraft is the Boeing B-17 Flying Fortress which the group operated during its stay at Grafton Underwood.

The Celtic cross and Star of David represents the various religions of the members of the 384th.

The theme of the design of the window was born of an idea by John Mach of Savannah, Georgia (related to a member of the group), and has been provided by the veterans, families and friends of the 384th Bombardment Group (Heavy). It was designed by Brian Thomas, OBE, who is a fellow of the British Society of Master Glass Painters, and has held distinguished office in many institutions associated with his craft. He has designed stained glass works for St Paul's Cathedral and Westminster Abbey, London, and Wellington Cathedral, New Zealand, as well as many memorials including those at Winchester Cathedral and

St George's Chapel, Windsor. The stained glass has been crafted and painted and the window assembled by Chapel Studios, specialist craftsmen in stained glass of Hunton Bridge, Hertfordshire, England.

A picture of the stained glass window was presented to the American Department of Defense and hangs in an entrance stairwell of the Pentagon in Washington DC. Another copy is in the World War II chapel at Hill Air Force Base, Ogden, Utah, USA.

The Memorial on the Geddington Road.

We saw in the church porch a plaque which tells of the avenue of trees that was being planted along the site of the old main runway as a memorial to the personnel who served on the station during the Second World War. One set of trees on the runway was given by the Daughters of the American Revolution — these were planted in memory of the personnel who died just before Christmas a few years ago when an American transport plane taking them home for Christmas crashed in Alaska. For the last seven years the villagers and the Americans have been replacing trees that had been taken down in 1942 to make way for the main runway.

One of the many hassocks with a World War II theme in the church of St James.

The airfield.
(from the village leaflet.)

Following the involvement of the United States in World War II the British and American Governments agreed that the British Government would provide port and airfield facilities and in return the American Government would supply Britain with arms.

A B17 Flying Fortress on the runway at Grafton Underwood during the Second World War. (With grateful thanks to Quentin Bland)

An airfield had been constructed just to the north of Grafton Underwood as a satellite airfield to the nearby Polebrook airfield, and so intended to be available in the event of Polebrook becoming unserviceable due to enemy action.

Built by George Wimpey and Co. Ltd. in 1941, improvements were made throughout the period of World War II. The airfield covered approximately 500 acres and during its construction two avenues of trees were destroyed along with many hedgerows and the houses and buildings of Rectory Farm and Grafton Lodge Farm.

The airfield was bisected by the Grafton to Brigstock road and, travelling north, the site of the airfield itself was to the left and the living domestic areas to the right. Full use was made of natural woodland for camouflage. The living area consisted mainly of wood and canvas hut construction, the more permanent buildings being brick built mess halls and clubs. The whole site accommodated up to 3,000 personnel and had all the facilities needed including a hospital, cinema and chapel.

The 384th, during its two years at Grafton, built up an enviable reputation and amongst its many achievements were two Divisional Unit Citations for Heroism and Dedication to Duty against Extreme Odds; over 1,000 personnel received the DFC. They achieved 9,348 credited sorties by their B17 Flying Fortresses, losing 159 aircraft and 1,579 personnel, but claiming 165 enemy aircraft.

Trail 4
Rockingham • Gretton • Great Oakley • Little Oakley • Brigstock • Sudborough • Drayton Park & Lowick

Rockingham

WHAT a delightful place to visit! We looked around the castle during a Craft Fair one Saturday.

The Saxons used this site for a stronghold, and in 1066 William the Conqueror ordered a castle to be built. This had a double role: it was an administration centre and also a hunting lodge for Rockingham Forest.

The castle hit troubled times during the Civil War and it fell to the Roundheads. Fortunately the hall and massive gateway still survive.

The impressive entrance to Rockingham Castle.

The Watson family have been in residence since 1530 (Commander and Mrs Saunders Watson are the residents now.). Charles Dickens used to visit the castle and dedicated *David Copperfield* to his friends Mr and Mrs Watson, the owners at the time. 'Chesney Wold' in *Bleak House* is loosely based on the castle.

A little story from George's book is worth telling here:

> Returning home in the fading dusk, I am reminded in climbing Rockingham Hill of the many stories woven round this steep, winding ascent. One I remember was a bet made by a well-known rider that he would ride his

Rockingham Castle; the Courtyard.
The Norman Great Hall, with front door added by Edward I, and Elizabethan windows.

penny-farthing up this famous hill, an almost super-human task. He did, however, succeed in his task, and in winning his bet, but it was not found out till much later that he sat on his machine in a wagon, which was drawn by four horses.

George was very fond of the village which is well worth visiting – it is just a short walk down the hill from the castle.

Oh! lovely realm of rich repose,
Deep set in verdant fields of green,
With noble trees, and garden close,
And dimpled hillocks dark between,
Small paths that wander where they will,
By shadowed copse and cool recess,
Go seeking sweeter pastures still,
Through deeper vales of loveliness.

The Courtyard seen from the Tower.

Gretton

GRETTON is a delightful village perched on the side of the Welland Valley. The old stocks and whipping post are authentically restored on the village green. The church (p. 42) is dedicated to St James and possesses a lovely square tower. There are signs of the Normans in the north arcade.

Close by is Kirby Hall, a marvellous Elizabethan structure saved from destruction by the then Ministry of Works. Inigo Jones did a lot of work here.

We would like to link George's view across the Welland Valley (p. 42) with our view of the marvellous piece of architecture known as the Welland Viaduct (p. 43) built to carry the old LMS line from Kettering to Oakham. It has 82 spans each 40 feet wide — really worth a visit any time you are Corby bound.

The Church of St James, Gretton.

The Welland Valley from Gretton.

The Welland Viaduct.

The Bridge over Harper's Brook at Great Oakley.

Great Oakley

Leafy lanes and sunlit gardens
Stand by meadows cool and sweet,
Steals the fragrant scent of clover
Even to the village street.

WE came to Great Oakley, now just saved from being swallowed up in the Corby Town sprawl. Alas!, the bridge that George drew (p. 43) is no more.

The great Mid-Tudor hall stands in the park with the church close by — worth a visit just to see the striking low pitched roof. Some of the stalls in the church

The manor house adjoining Little Oakley church was the home of the Montagu family, now a farmhouse. There has not been a lot of change since George did this sketch.

Great Oakley church, dedicated to St Michael.

came from Pipewell Abbey. The abbey has now vanished but there is a very unusual church in Pipewell, said to have been built from the stones of the abbey. The church is very small, in the shape of a crucifix, with no aisles and no pews, and with a little squat tower. The village of Pipewell gained its name from a nearby spring.

Little Oakley

WE visited Little Oakley on a fortuitous day, when the Orton Trust, whose workshops are in the redundant church of St Peter, were in the throes of repairing the shrine of St Alban.

Little Oakley.

The bridge at Little Oakley is no more, replaced by one of concrete. But to get the view that George drew we had to move up the road slightly as the cottages are now hidden by a large weeping willow.

The Orton Trust is a training centre for stone and ornamental masons. They train at both Orton church and at Little Oakley, but are soon to vacate Little Oakley. However, we understand that St Peter's will still be used for training of another sort, thought to be carpentry.

The shrine of St Albans had been badly repaired in the Victorian times and was falling to pieces and had to be repaired before it was lost forever. The church is leased to Colin Hill and Paul Harrison Co. who are monumental masons and specialise in restoration work.

The Orton Trust Pamphlet states:

> The Orton Trust was founded in 1968 with the aim of encouraging the traditional stonemasonry skills used in the restoration and conservation of historical buildings. Its activities are based on the redundant church at Orton near Kettering.
>
> The trust made a further contribution to the re-use of redundant churches when in 1977 it acquired St Peter's, Little Oakley near Corby which is leased to other companies in the masonry business.

Brigstock

By leafy woods, clear streams and pastures
Far from the noise of town,
The village stands, serene and olden,
With cobbled streets and pathways brown,
Where to the fields the carts and wagons
Go creaking up and down.

B RIGSTOCK is deep in the heart of Rockingham Forest. The noble church of St Andrew has a rugged Saxon tower, which was heightened a stage in the fourteenth century and topped by a spire in the fifteenth. There is much fine woodwork in the church, medieval and modern, and a marble effigy of the Lord Lyveden who was Secretary for War at the opening of the Crimean campaign.

Harper's Brook runs through the village, which is named after the bridge over the brook. By the village green is an Elizabethan Cross carved in memory of Queen Elizabeth I, Queen Anne and Queen Victoria.

George Harrison.

The church of St Andrew was built by the Saxons in a clearing in the middle of the forest. It was a safe refuge from the marauding tribes and the Danish

Brigstock Cross.

Upon the Market Cross the letters
Carved for a gracious queen,
Remain to stir the mind with visions
Of all that time has seen
Since Drake sailed west to fight and conquer
Where none but Drake had been.

invaders. The church has a fifteenth century porch, a 700 year old doorway and a Saxon turret at the side of the tower.

The scene at Brigstock is the same today as when George sat here all those years ago except that Harper's Brook has dug its channel deeper.

Sudborough.

With the road on the ridge it was difficult to arrive at the same scene that George drew – so we photographed the Church of All Saints, Sudborough from the village street.

Sudborough

I see the smoke from Corby chimneys
Float lazily across the sky,
The puffs of dust on Lowick high road
Before the breeze go drifting by,
And cornfields, streams, and wide flat meadows
In summer's shim'ring white heat lie.

SUDBOROUGH is only a mile or two from the confluence of Harper's Brook and the River Nene. From the high ground nearby one can see far over the forest to the tall chimneys at Corby (*these belonged to Corby steel works, now demolished*). There are still relics of the forest near Sudborough, notably King Stephen's Ride; the fishponds of old monasteries also remain. In the thirteenth and fourteenth century church is the monument to Robert de Vere, who went to the crusades of 1249 as standard bearer to William de Longsword. Robert de Vere fell with his leader, and is commemorated here by the oldest armoured figure in any English Church.

George Harrison

Drayton Park & Lowick

LOWICK in olden times was known as Luffwick. It is entered in the *Domesday Book* as Lukwic. The village is situated two miles north of Thrapston and is the last village on Harper's Brook.

Drayton House: The Front Entrance.

The lovely church of St Peter is mainly Perpendicular. The large octagonal lantern on the tower is a striking feature around the countryside — it rises from a battlemented parapet of the tower.

We went through the village to visit Drayton House to photograph the front entrance of the house which George sketched. The house is the home of Mr L. G. Stopford Sackville whom we thank for permission to take the photograph.

We thought you would like to read George's description of his visit:

The approach through a beautiful wooded park, with avenues of elms and lime, gives a regal appearance to the house.

The most wonderful thing about Drayton is the way its antiquity has been preserved, for it is a house that is continually lived in.

It has seen a curious interchange among families, owing to the fact that it has descended several times to heiresses: but throughout its interesting eight hundred years history it has never been sold, or even let.

Seen from the Thrapston approach the building is remarkably picturesque, with its two towers crowned with cupolas, while to the right is the formal garden, rich with old-world flowers, backed by hedges of hornbeam.

Our view of Drayton House.

On this grey February day Lowick was a village of quiet peacefulness. I could hear, borne on the west wind, the dim sounds of traffic from the main road. Cattle were lowing in the fields and birds were singing their first tremulous songs of spring in the church close. Its very quietness (for these sounds but made the quiet quieter) seemed to sink into my soul, and I wondered "Will the inevitable advance of speed and wheels rob us in time of these peaceful sanctuaries, or shall we act in time to save for us and for the generations yet to be, some of the beauties which have been to all our people a sacred heritage, and the source of all that is lovely in our national life?"

Where have we heard that before?

Trail 5
Deene Park • Bulwick • King's Cliffe • Duddington • Collyweston

Deene Park

DEENE has been for me an inspiration, a source of loveliness enjoyed through many years of quiet peace. I was scarcely out of my teens when I was first privileged to sketch in the park and by the lake.

I remember the morning so clearly as if it was yesterday, so distinctly is its superlative loveliness imprinted upon memory. It was late May. Beneath the trees was a mist of blue forget-me-nots, tall parsleys, and golden kingcups. The trees threw quaint shadows across this space of flowers,

Deene Hall: The Porch.

which changed from deep blue to glowing amber. A King Emperor butterfly settled on a reed before me, opening and closing his marvellously coloured wings in the warmth of the spring sunlight. He stayed long enough for me to admire his wonderful markings before flying away. The lake shimmering in the light of morning, reflecting the passing delicately-tinted clouds upon its unruffled surface, where various aquatic birds disported themselves with the joy of life, and the swallows swooped down to seize the unsuspecting fly, to leave for a moment a gleam of silver, caught by the sun's rays, where the pointed wings had touched the water. Behind me an old stone wall flickered in hue with the varying tones of sun and shadow, and beyond, with the spire light against the blue of sky, stood the church, the last resting place of Lord Cardigan, nestling between its ancient trees.

Our view of the doorway (by kind permission of Mr & Mrs E Brudenell).

To most people of Northamptonshire, and indeed to many beyond this county, Deene is associated with the name of Lord Cardigan, the hero of the famous Balaclava charge, and of his Countess, who, until her death in 1915, made Deene Hall her home.

The last earl was the seventh of his line, and represented the tenth generation of the Brudenells of Deene. Sir Robert Brudenell rose to be one of the judges of the King's Bench under Henry VIII. He bought the manor in 1518. His grandson Sir Edmond was the first to carry out serious building operations at Deene. His first wife was a Bussey of Lincolnshire. The Brudenells were proud of this alliance, and their arms with those of Bussey are found on the porch by which the quadrangle is entered from the north.

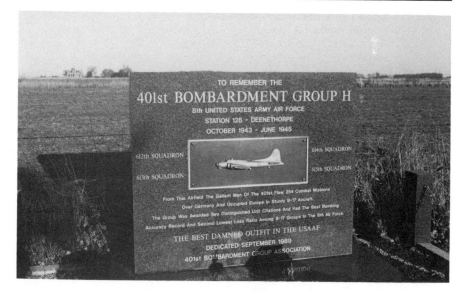

During World War II there was an American airfield nearby. This memorial now remembers the men of the USAAF who were stationed here. 'The best damned outfit in the USAAF'.

Sir Edmond's nephew was created Lord Brudenell in 1627 and Earl of Cardigan in 1661.

The church was almost entirely rebuilt by the late Countess of Cardigan in memory of her first husband, the Balaclava hero.

George Harrison

Bulwick

WE came to Bulwick in the early summer and found it a lovely village as we sat on the hill overlooking Willow Brook.

Bulwick is the seat of the Tryon family, distinguished soldiers and sailors (more about them on our visit to Collyweston). There are many memorials to them in the church of St Nicholas. This church had a famous rector around 1849 (as Whellan's *History, Gazetteer and Directory of Northamptonshire, 1849* tells us). He was the Revd. F. Tryon and he had in his possession more than a hundred coins from the period of Julius Caesar; and more than that number of Saxon and Monastic coins, found in the parish, as well as a seal of Pope Urbanus V which he found in one of the rectorial fields and which is thought to have been appended to some document belonging to one of the neighbouring monasteries. This parish being contiguous to the great forest of Rockingham, it was a favourite station for both Saxons and Romans – and monks also, the forest at that time being well stocked with deer, so providing a good supply of venison.

Bulwick.

The stately church stands dim against the sky,
In tender lines of symmetry and grace;
The evening breezes croon a lullaby
Through lofty trees, that darkly interlace
And cast dim shadows through the narrow street
Where meadow fields and old world gardens meet.

King's Cliffe

KING'S CLIFFE sits overlooking the valley of the Willow Brook. This is a division of Rockingham Forest and many of the houses are tiled in Collyweston slate.

A magnificent Norman tower rises from the church surmounted by a spire added in 1220. Parts of the pulpit and the beautiful fifteenth century bench ends came from Rockingham Castle.

In the eighteenth century a very pious theologian lived here named William Law. He greatly impressed John Wesley who was thereby inspired to found the Methodist church.

George's description of his visit in 1946:

Upon entering King's Cliffe I am at once struck by the curiously stunted appearance of the spire of the church. Upon climbing the opposite hill I get

King's Cliffe, with All Saints' Church

The scene today, with the cottage on the corner being renovated.

a bird's eye view of the village with its long line of houses stretching for some distance along the valley, and of the graceful curve of the railway on its northern slope. The valley is watered by a small stream, Willow Brook, out of which the fish ponds have been formed; and up at Blatherwyke the Deene lakes have been developed. After a winding journey the Brook finally unites with the Nene a short distance below Fotheringhay.

The history of the village called Clive and King's Clive, goes back to Saxon times, for in a battle in the vicinity in AD778, Ethelred, King of Northumbria was killed. At this time the village was but a few mud huts inhabited by fierce warriors. In the time of John it was owned by the King, and he had a Mansion here, hence the name King's Cliffe, the Cliffe being the steep slope on which the village is perched. When Henry III became king he gave Cliffe to his Queen.

Edward II and other Kings did likewise, and so it became Queens' property. Later it was bought by a Lord Burleigh, whose descendants were Lords of the Manor. Most historians agree that at one time King's Cliffe was an important town.

Duddington

WE had visited this village twice before and were impressed by its simple beauty. It has been saved from the devastation of vehicle traffic by two by-passes, the A47 re-routed north of the village and the A43 to the east, and now tranquillity reigns — as this village well deserves.

Church of St Mary, Duddington. The roses that Arthur Mee remarked upon in 1945 are still here!

We are following here not only in George's footsteps but also in those of another traveller, Arthur Mee, who wrote that remarkable series of books *The King's England*. In his notes on Duddington he says "We found roses climbing over the massive church door trying to reach the tower" — as you can see times do not change in this lovely place. The medieval mill still stands, although renovated, just as George sketched it all those years ago.

We have found what could be a useful bit of information for the residents of

Duddington Mill.

Duddington Mill is little changed today.

Duddington in Whellan's *History, Gazetteer and Directory of Northamptonshire, 1849*:

"By virtue of a charter, granted in the reign of Elizabeth I, the inhabitants of Duddington, are toll free throughout the kingdom."

So if you are a resident and you travel over the Severn bridge, the Humber bridge or the Dartford tunnel and bridge, they should be free to you — if you can persuade the authorities to let you through. Good luck!

Collyweston

OUR visit to Collyweston was on a lovely sunny summer's day. The village stands near the end of the Northamptonshire heights which are a continuation of the Cotswold Hills — their elevation above sea level is over 700ft in the south west, declining to 300ft near Collyweston.

It was the home of the Collyweston slate mines, worked for a long time, but production ceased in 1967. We asked a local builder who specialises in the slate why it had stopped: he said that although there still were a couple of mines that could be worked, mining has to be done in the winter months to allow severe frosts to split the slates — and we do not have winters severe enough these days to make it viable. He now uses recycled slates from old barns, etc.[‡]

Browsing through the Northamptonshire archives we came across a bit of Collyweston history.

"Throughout the years the name has been used as a metaphor for being awry or out of square or crooked, e.g. a hat put on anyhow was, to Mary Webb in 1916, 'all a Collywesson'. A ladder that has seen better days was called 'Collywisth'd'. The saying probably came from the way the roofs used to bend under the weight of the tiles.

Some other uses were:
Shropshire (1841): All a lung a Connyweston — a bonnet put on awkwardly.
Cheshire: It's gone a bit Collyweston — when things go wrong.
Northamptonshire: It's all along o' Collyweston — when things go wrong.
Lancashire (1855): Everything goes Collywest — lost or damaged.
Lincolnshire (1866): He's a bit Collywesson — he's a bit contrary.
Lancashire (1875): Never mind, he ne'er agrees with anyone. He's awluz Collywest — in the other way or opposite direction."

In the Second World War Collyweston had an airfield and was the home of Flight 1426 which had the task of evaluating captured and crashed enemy aircraft. These were repaired and then flown around British airfields in order to familiarise British and US aircrews with their appearance. (*Grateful thanks to Stan Weston of Kettering for this piece of information.*)

[‡]   We recently learned that two enterprising gentlemen had re-started the production of Collyweston slates. They first soak the stone with water and then place it into one of two refrigeration units that they have installed. The freezing causes the stone to split just as it did traditionally by the effect of frost.

As far as we can discover this is still in the experimental stage as it is difficult to reproduce even today what nature does normally. But we wish them good luck.

Collyweston.

The scene today is virtually unchanged from when George came here.

Trail 6

Weldon • Benefield • Wansford • Fotheringhay • Cotterstock

Weldon

WELDON was once known as 'Weldon in the Woods': this explains why the church has a cupola on the tower — a lamp was placed in here at night so that travellers and workers in Rockingham Forest could find their way...

Now glows the sun upon the old church tower,
On vaulted lamp, on glass that glints and gleams.
Oft in the darkness of the midnight hour,
The toilers have been guided by its beams.

St Mary's Church and Lantern Tower, Weldon.

It is well known for the quarries of Weldon stone, famous for its building strength and used extensively throughout the country.

The church is dedicated to St Mary and is mostly Early English and Perpendicular and was probably built by the Bassets, former owners of Weldon. The church originally had a spire, but this fell down when some repairs were being carried out. Old maps show the existence of the spire in 1630.

St Mary's Church today.

The 'Corby kiln', which is believed to belong to the Romano-British period (AD43 to AD410), was discovered here. It was found by accident by ironstone workers.

Benefield

THIS is a village in two parts — Upper and Lower Benefield. We had to come to Lower Benefield to find George's lovely lych-gate at the church dedicated

The beautiful lych-gate at the Church to the Blessed Virgin.

to The Blessed Virgin. The miserere stalls in the church came from Fotheringhay: close by the church a castle used to stand.

The Lych Gate as George saw it.

This ancient Lych Gate, symbol of repose
Between the busy world and life's long close,
Brings to the tired heart the hope of rest,
The faith, through love, in one who knoweth best.

Wansford

WHEN George visited this village it was still in Northamptonshire but now it has been stolen by Cambridgeshire!

It was at Wansford that we heard the story associated with the inn by the river called 'The Haycock'. It seems that a traveller named Barnabee was passing through the county and rested the night at Wansford. As a plague was raging at the time he decided to sleep in a field by the Nene on a haycock (a

The old bridge at Wansford.

Wansford Bridge is still as beautiful as ever.

pile of hay). During the night there was a flood and he was carried off in his sleep. He was swept downstream, still asleep, towards Wisbech in the Fens; he was seen and taken up by some fishermen, almost in the open sea, and on being asked where he lived, answered "at Wansford in England". The lovely old coaching inn was named after this incident.

The date on the inn shows 1632. It was a favourite stopping off place for the north and south coaches.

Also, as recorded by Arthur Mee, the Haycock was one of the first hotels in England to provide a landing stage for private aircraft. The church across the river was founded by the Saxons.

A Riverside Landing.

Fotheringhay Bridge with the Church of The Blessed Virgin Mary and All Saints.

Fotheringhay

WE visited this beautiful village, nestling close to the River Nene, on numerous occasions. It is another of our villages steeped in history and once had a castle where Mary, Queen of Scots was imprisoned and beheaded. We do not have the space here to write of her stay but if you go to your public

This old doorway was originally the entrance to the New Inn, Fotheringhay.

library and consult Whellan's *History, Gazetteer and Directory of Northamptonshire, 1849* you will find there a graphic description of the events leading up to her execution.

All that is left of the castle is part of the moat and a large piece of masonry surrounded by a railing, close to the Nene. If you look around the grounds in the summer months you may see some large thistles growing — it is said that these are the descendants of the seeds Mary, Queen of Scots brought with her from Scotland and planted in the grounds during her long imprisonment.

George's visit is described thus:

> The approach to the village from this direction is beautiful indeed. On this peaceful August afternoon, with the warm haze quivering over the meadowlands, I am impressed with the pastoral beauty that lies around me. The Nene, full to its reedy banks, owing to the abnormal summer rains, reflects the limpid bowl of sky above like a mirror; the flat meadowlands,

George's sketch of the old doorway, Fotheringhay.

delightfully green where sleek cattle stand knee-deep in the scented grass; the tall reeds now in flower lining the river's banks, with here and there a patch of bright colour from willow herb, spearwort, and ragged robin; and the bridge to the right delicately reflected in the water, a symbol of many years of usefulness. This eighteenth-century bridge over the Nene is one of the most considerable in the county.

Looking across to Fotheringhay from the Nene. The castle mound is on the right.

In the glory of the morning
Shines the sun on Fotheringhay,
Gilding far the sleepy river,
And with gold the meadow way...

Cotterstock

WHAT a beautiful place to stop on our journeying! — we can now see why George liked it so much. Standing on the Nene side is the lovely church of St Andrew. It's a bit of a mixture — the tower is of several architectural periods; the west door is Norman, the upper stages date from the thirteenth century, and the battlements are from the fifteenth century.

John Dryden visited here twice in his old age. Look around and see Cotterstock Hall, built in 1658, and the beautiful restored mill, a lovely quiet corner of England, echoed in one of George's poems:

The white wreathed hedgerows at Springtime,
The autumn's ripe corn in the ear,
A bird's sweet song in the gloaming,
The presence of beauty near.

The Church of St Andrew, Cotterstock

...and as we found it.

Trail 7
Oundle • Barnwell • Pilton • Aldwincle

Oundle

WE love to visit this beautiful town, with its buildings of stone and Collyweston tiles, which nestles in a lovely bend of the River Nene. It is known to have existed for at least a thousand years, its markets and tolls having been confirmed by King Edgar in AD972. Its narrow streets with their tiny cottages, many alleyways and narrow yards are now protected from traffic by a by-pass. If George were to come back today he would not see a lot of difference. Let us hope that it remains unspoilt!

St Osyth's Lane, Oundle

The town contains many old inns, notably the Talbot Inn which is reputed to be 300 years old. The large window on the lovely oak staircase came from the Hall of Fotheringhay Castle.

The church of St Peter has a fine crocketed spire, a richly ornamented fifteenth century porch and a pre-Reformation pulpit. It stands in the centre of the town among the buildings of the famous Oundle School, founded by a London grocer, William Laxton, born in the sixteenth century, who became Lord Mayor of London.

Here stands in splendour still the ancient school,
So wise in precept for each golden rule,
Once small in outlook, and unknown to fame,
It now has grown to bear an honoured name.

Alas! St Osyth's Lane has lost some houses for — guess what? Yes, a car park! But at least it's free!

Courtyard, The Talbot Inn. (You will find this little changed.)

Barnwell

Blooms now the cowslip and the dainty smock,
The white-eyed speedwell's swimming mist of blue.
The dandelions in deeper splendour mock
The waving buttercups' less golden hue,
And every hedgerow flaunts its wreath of may,
Soft, fairy snow-drifts in the light of day.

Barnwell Mill

...now restored as a restaurant.

WE agree with George about the many fine views around this village. The old Mill is now tastefully restored as a restaurant – a picture that has not changed over the years.

Barnwell is a village of two parishes. Once known as Barnwell St Andrew and Barnwell All Saints, only the chancel is left of All Saints, but this is well worth a visit to see the memorials to the Montagu family.

It was in this village that we met a wonderful lady called Paddy Kitchen who has written several books, one on her own village called *Barnwell*. We are now good friends and every time we visit there's always an open door to welcome us.

At the St Andrews end of the village is the castle and the manor house, the country seat of the Duke and Duchess of Gloucester.

Barnwell Castle was built by Berengar le Moigne in the reign of Henry I (1132). In the fourth year of Edward 1 (1276) Beregarius le Moigne sold it together with the manor to William, Abbot of Ramsey, in the county of Huntingdon, to which abbey it belonged until the general suppression in the reign of Henry VIII. Sir Edward Montagu, Lord Chief Justice of the Kings Bench, purchased it from that monarch in 1540 and repaired it and beautified it, and it subsequently became the Baronial residence of his noble descendants.

One story of interest in Whellan's *History, Gazetteer and Directory of Northamptonshire,* 1849:

> "On the 17th June 1721 a heavy rain accompanied with thunder and lightning inundated the village, the water rising to the height of five to six feet in the houses. Drowned several sheep, and in the subsiding, carried a wagon laden with wood along with it for 200 yards."

The church of All Saints was pulled down in 1821, except for the chancel which was kept as a mausoleum of the Earl of Sandwich, a branch of the noble family of Montagu. There is a lovely pyramidical monument to a young son who tragically drowned. Well worth a visit, the key can be obtained from a house close by.

Pilton

A LOVELY poem by George sums up this tranquil place. The church stands in a meadow close to the Manor House: it was in this church that Erasmus Dryden was married. His son was Poet Laureate to James II. Close by is the beautiful village of Wadenhoe, well worth a visit. Do not miss the church, set aside from the village on the hill overlooking the Nene.

I never walk these narrow lanes,
Nor see the fields afar,
But I can feel how lovely still
These homeland beauties are.

Sometimes the scent of April rains
Makes fragrant every breeze,
The wet grass glimmers where the sun
Strikes downwards through the trees.

The Nene, looking towards Pilton.

Aldwincle

A GAIN we visit a twin village — two churches, All Saints and St Peter, All Saints now sadly redundant. The spelling of the name of the village seems to be optional — Aldwincle or Aldwinkle. We have used the version adopted by the Ordnance Survey.

It was here in the rectory that John Dryden was born in 1631, his grandfather being the rector. He wrote comedies of rather a coarse nature "not for the ears of the gentry" but he was a great poet and writer. He died on May 1st 1700, and a hundred carriage cortège followed his coffin to Westminster Abbey.

Another great writer, Thomas Fuller, was born here in 1608. He lived in the village and was a staunch loyalist — during the Civil War he wrote his most famous work *Worthies of England*. He was also a popular preacher. He died in 1661 in Cranford, Middlesex.

We would like you to read George's account of his visit — it sums up the area very well:

I never visit this part of the Nene without being charmed by its quiet simplicity, its wealth of flowers, its varied grasses, and reeds, with an abundance of wild life, which add to the music of the low murmur of the waters lapping the bending reeds. This beautiful river scenery stretches from Aldwincle to Wadenhoe. Its unique charm lies in the circuitous winding of the river, and the lush quality of the willow fringed flat meadow lands. Here is a corner of Northamptonshire where the lover of nature may dream through the sultry noon conscious only of sounds that soothe, of moving colour, the scent of flowers, and the sweet content of musing in a world where all is peace.

The Old Dryden Rectory, Aldwincle.

The thatch has now gone from the Dryden Rectory – it was replaced by Collyweston slate in 1971. (This must have been re-cycled slate – see Collyweston in Trail 5.)

Trail 8

Great Addington • Irthlingborough • Irchester • Wellingborough • Great Doddington • Earls Barton

Great Addington

ON this particular October afternoon the Nene Valley lay bathed in the glorious sunlight of early autumn. Where the corn had been lately carried, the stubble fields rolled away like ribbons of old gold, against the deep green of pasture lands.

Arriving at Great Addington I was met by Mrs Barritt, late of Kettering, who introduced me to the Rector, the Rev. D. H. Meggy, who graciously conducted me round the church, and allowed me to view the register which had been entirely re-written by a former rector, the Rev. Thomas Cox, from the original which came to light in an old farmhouse, partly gnawed away by rats. The church is dedicated to All Saints. The tomb of Sir Henry Vere, with an alabaster effigy, is sixteenth century. The work is beautifully executed, and of special interest as representing the harness in which he fought at Bosworth.

It will be noticed that the legs are straight and not crossed, denoting that he had not visited the Holy Land.

The Church of All Saints, Great Addington.

In the twilight of an autumn day I walked back to Woodford, and saw the Nene Valley enfolded in the pearly greys of coming night. The little trains were cutting through the tender colour, and the twinkling lights of Ringstead and Thrapston sending out their rays like bright stars, and the Nene mirroring the hue of sky.

George Harrison

Irthlingborough

WE saw the striking tower from the new by-pass as we approached. St Peter's church has this lovely tower which, at the end of the last century, was taken down stone by stone as it was leaning over by at least 30 inches. Each stone was numbered as it was removed and the tower was then

The Tower of St Peter's Church, Irthlingborough

...and today.

rebuilt, taking nearly six years to complete. The church itself was built around the end of the fourteenth century by John Pyel, a merchant who became Lord Mayor of London in 1373. The tower rises to 99 feet.

A few notes from George:

At Irthlingborough we touch the industrial area of the county. With Higham Ferrers on the hill to our left, close by is the confluence of the Ise and Nene. The Ise is a pleasant stream which comes down from the high ground near Naseby. The Second Duke of Montagu used its waters to make Boughton Park into a smaller but beautiful Versailles; his water gardens are gone, but today the Ise feeds the lake at Wicksteed Park, Kettering, which is a source of joy to oarsmen, pleasure boaters, owners of model launches and of course the children.

The Ise in Flood.

Wellingborough

Viewed from some distant breezy hill,
With pleasant pastures spread below,
With here and there a farm, a mill,
A remnant of the long ago,
The town lies like an isle of dreams,
Beyond a tree-fringed cool recess,
Where every farther stage but seems
A sweeter vale of loveliness.

ONCE the home of the Abbots of Croyland, Wellingborough was, in olden times, well known for its lace making. It is mentioned in the *Domesday Book* and was granted market rights by King John in 1201.

All around the town centre are pieces of old Wellingborough. There is a lovely thatched restaurant, and just up the hill is The Hind, a seventeenth century coaching inn where Cromwell stayed on his way to Naseby during the Civil War. The Georgian mansion in Swanspool gardens is now council offices.

Swanspool Gardens, Wellingborough.

Wellingborough suffered from fire in 1738 and the town was then rebuilt.

It was famous for the Red Well spring with its water 'of highly medicinal virtue', and was also known for 'Whittens embrocation', manufactured in the town and distributed all over the kingdom, famous for 'its healing and beneficial effects, both to human and brute creation'.

Before you leave Wellingborough do visit the Tithe Barn, a beautiful restored barn once belonging to Grange Farm that used to stand behind the Hind Inn.

The church in the town centre is dedicated to All Hallows: parts of it are some 600 years old and it contains some attractive modern stained-glass windows. The tower with its broach spire rises to a height of 165 ft. The church was extensively restored in 1843 and recently repaired.

The Church of All Hallows, Wellingborough.

Irchester

No stately towers their tender shadows cast
On ancient court yards or on green retreats,
Yet round thy cottage homes sweet peace abides,
Grown lovely through the passing years of time.

A NOTHER historic spot. The Romans settled hereabouts, and when iron ore was being mined a Saxon cemetery was found in which 400 Saxons were buried, all facing East.

The spire of St Katherine's soars to a height of 156 feet. There are signs of Norman work about the church.

The gravestones in front of the altar are of the Jenyson family. A son, Thomas, left money for loaves to be distributed to the poor, and the church once had a shelf on which the loaves were stored.

The Spire of St Katherine's Church, Irchester.

Great Doddington

A village set beyond the grey
Dull monotone of busy town,
With meadow fields that melt away
To meet the uplands, gold and brown.

FROM here you have great views over the Nene Valley as Great Doddington sits up on the valley-side. The view in olden times looked out on ironstone workings — now we have sand and gravel excavations.

The Norman church of St Nicholas has as its companion a 600 year old yew tree in the churchyard.

View from Great Doddington — Evening.

Earls Barton

Dear winding paths by shady lanes,
That lie in distance scarce a mile,
And further still the uplands rise
With half the green world spread below,
Where sweep the changing English skies,
And pure unfettered breezes blow.

HERE stands one of Northamptonshire's most historic churches. Dedicated to All Saints, the tower is Saxon and most of the body is Norman. The mound to the rear of the church is all that remains of a Norman castle.

An interesting local story concerns workmen employed on the tower in 1934 who found a horse's tooth embedded in a wall. It is thought that this could be associated with pagan beliefs that led to horses heads being built into the walls of temples.

George writes:

> Earls Barton was the scene of the early ministry of William Carey of Paulerspury, near Towcester. He preached here in 1782-3, before being ordained as a Baptist Minister at Moulton, a few miles away.
>
> It may well be that the beauty of Earls Barton church was not without a lasting affect on Carey. He certainly carried with him to India a profound realisation of the moral value of great architecture, and he left behind him, in Serampore College, one of the most beautiful University buildings in the Orient.

The Church of All Saints, Earls Barton.

Trail 9
Northampton

We have touched on Northampton only briefly, but to get a better look we suggest that you read 'Northampton, A Guided Tour' by Tony Noble (Meridian Books). He takes you on a fine walk around this most interesting town.

A UGUST Bank Holiday Monday, 1989 was a particularly important day for the town, for it then celebrated the 800 year charter given to the town by Richard I in 1189. (p. 86)

We are grateful to the Northampton Archive Department at Wooton Hall for the photostat of the old Charter (p. 86). We apologise for the poor quality of the print. The Charter is a very old document — it has to be treated with extreme care and could not be re-photographed for us.

The Charter is in abbreviated Latin – here is a translation of part of it:

Richard by the grace of God, King of England, Duke of Normandy and Aquitaine, Count of Anjou. To the Archbishops, Bishops, Abbots, Earls, Barons, Justices, Sheriffs and all his ministers and faithful men, French and English, greetings. Know that we have granted to our burgesses of Northampton that none of them plead outside the walls of the borough of Northampton on any plea besides pleas relating to external tenures except our moneyers and ministers. Also we have granted to them quittance of the murder fine within the borough and its liberties and that none of them make duel and that of pleas pertaining to the Crown they may justify according to the custom of the citizens of the City of London.

(With grateful thanks to the Northampton Record Office.)

George, in his book, reaches Northampton at the end of a cruise along the River Nene:

Now the river valley is narrowing greatly, and soon we are at the confluence of the North and South Nene, and must end our cruise, for above Northampton the river is no longer navigable. But we have fallen in love with

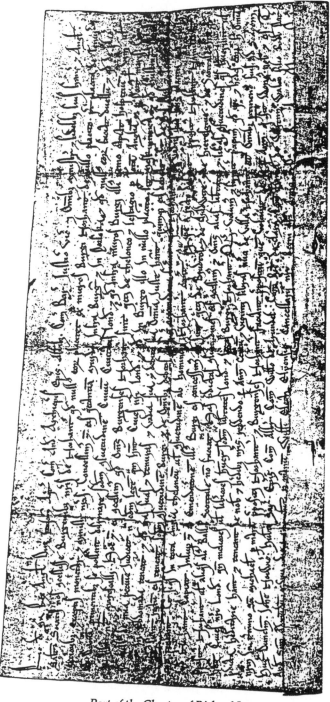

Part of the Charter of Richard I.

the Nene, and as the ordnance map dignifies the southern, not the northern, stream with the name 'River Nene', we will follow it by road after an evening walk to Hunsbury Hill and a night at The Angel, Northampton, which Inn is mentioned in the Borough Rental of 1504. (*The Angel is in Bridge Street.*)
...

From the Conquest to the reign of King Henry III, Northampton was the seat of a mint, the coins of which like those of Southampton bore the mint letters HAM, HAMTU, HAMTUN, except that some later Northampton coins were stamped NORHAM or an abbreviation thereof. From the Conquest to the Restoration the town had walls and a Royal Castle, where Court and Parliament often sat; but as punishment for the town's vigorous support of the Parliamentary cause, Charles II ordered the destruction of the walls and the dismantling of the Castle, which was finally destroyed in 1880. The Castle stood on the grounds of Castle Station Goods Yard, with the North Nene as its defence on one side.

Northampton from Hunsbury Hill.

When the town was burned down in 1675, the Earl of Northampton dashed over from Castle Ashby, organised the fire-fighting, and afterwards provided for the relief of distress. This prompt action saved the three fine churches of St Giles, St Peter's and St Sepulchre's, the last being one of the three remaining Round Churches built by returned Crusaders on the plan of the Church of the Holy Sepulchre at Jerusalem. All Saints' Church was damaged but rebuilt by Wren.

It is fitting that Northampton which for centuries has stood in the forefront of the battle for religious and political freedom, should have been the ancestral home of both parents of George Washington, first President of the

United States of America and 'Father of his Country'. The portrait and Arms of Laurence Washington, Mayor in 1532-3 and 1545-6, are still preserved in the Town Hall, while the records of All Saints Church carry many items connected with the Elizabethan and Stuart forebears of George Washington's mother, Mary Ball.

Northampton has long been noted for its care of the young, the aged and the infirm. Today it is finely provided with schools, parks and gardens, and has delightful homes for the aged sponsored by the various religious bodies.

In his account George quotes from a description of Northampton dating from the time of George II:

Northampton is one of the prettiest Towns in England. It was burnt down Septr. 3d 1675 but soon rebuilt again much finer and more uniform than it was before. 'Tis a Borough Town: governed by a Mayor, Recorder, two Bailiffs, 4 Aldermen, 48 Common Council men, a Town Clerk, &c. Its 4 principal Streets open to the four Cardinal Points. 'Tis thought to have been a very ancient Town and is at present a place of great Trade. The Market Place which is esteem'd one of the Finest in Europe, is a spacious Square, ranged on every side with handsome houfses, and its Markets and Fairs Celebrated for the best Horses in the Kingdom. The County Gaol, Quarter Sefsions and Afsizes, are usually kept here. The chief Manufactures are Shoes and Stockings, and tho' it has no Commerce by Navigation yet 't is rich and populous. Here's a good free School, an Alms-house and lately erected by a generous Contribution an Infirmary for Sick and diseased poor people.

Images of Medieval times were conjured up during the festival commemorating the eight hundredth anniversary of the granting of Northampton's Charter in 1189.

While browsing round a book fair we came across a *Northampton Town Guide* of 1927 by Reginald W. Brown (Chief Librarian and Curator), published by the *Northampton Mercury*. In it we found a graphic description of the great fire of 1675.

The great fire of Northampton in 1675 seems to make a sharp dividing line between the old town of medieval times and the town as it exists today. There are several accounts of the disaster…

Carmen Funebre written in Latin by the Rev. Dr. S. Ford, describes the outbreak in the following lines:

A cottage poor there stood, at farthest West,
To poor a Covert, and a Nest;

The Seals of the Ancient Boroughs of Northamptonshire.
Centre: The Badge of Northampton.

Thatch'd overhead, and Thatch'd o' the floor,
With Straw and Litter, to the door;
A Barn, a Stable, or a Hog-stye whether?
Barn, Stable, Hog-stye, all-together.
A Wisp with Embers from a Neighbour fetched,
Blazing in hand, the Litter catch'd.
The Wind impetuous, at West-Nor-West,
The Door stood to the Wind, full brest.

Then later on in the same poem occurs the following spirited account:

Help here:- a Ladder quickly:- yonders Hook:-
O:- quickly, quickly:- Sirs, for God-sake look:
The Fire has here but new now took.

A view of Northampton's magnificent Guildhall
by our friend John Thomas Neville RIBA.

Some Buckets there:- What are your Stocks, or Stone!
Some Water, quickly, - or the house is gone!
What! - the Pumps burnt! - No Water any where! -
Go stave the Hogs-heads:- fetch up Pails of Beer!
Dash, - dash;- O quickly;- more;- more yet;- one here!-
(I charge you stand your Ground)- another there!
Five Pounds (good fellows) here, as a reward,
To stand your Centry sure, and keep, strict Guard
...

The fire began about noon near the Castle at the west end of town, at a thatched house in St. Mary's Street. The season had not been so dry for many years past and a high west wind was blowing.

So here we are at the end of this set of our trails around Northamptonshire. We hope you have enjoyed them as much as we have. We found some wonderful people on our trips, some of whom have become firm friends, and we look forward to meeting you again when we follow in George's footsteps further around the county in the not too distant future.

Thank you Northamptonshire for sharing your secrets and beauty, and, most of all, thank you George for opening our eyes to all the wonders about us.

Medieval minstrels at the Charter celebrations.

Index